ISSUES
OF OUR
TIME

DRUGS IN SOCIETY

Are They Our Suicide Pill?

John Salak

Twenty-First Century Books

**A Division of Henry Holt and Company
New York**

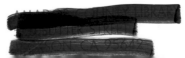

Twenty-First Century Books
A division of Henry Holt and Company, Inc.
115 West 18th Street
New York, New York 10011

©1993 by Blackbirch Graphics, Inc.
First Edition
5 4 3 2 1

Published in Canada by Fitzhenry & Whiteside Ltd.
195 Allstate Parkway, Markham, Ontario L3R 4T8

Printed in the United States of America

Created and produced in association with Blackbirch Graphics, Inc.

Photo Credits:
Cover: ©Stuart Rabinowitz/Blackbirch Graphics, Inc.; p. 4–5: ©Oscar Burriel/Latin Stock/Science Photo Library; p. 6: AP/Wide World Photos; p. 9: ©Dr. Jeremy Burgess/Science Photo Library; p. 13: North Wind Picture Archives; p. 15: AP/Wide World Photos; p. 16–17: ©Richard Hutchings/Photo Researchers, Inc.; p. 19: ©Carl Purcell/Photo Researchers, Inc.; p. 21: Gamma Liaison; p. 22: ©Jan Halaska/Photo Researchers Inc.; p. 24–25: ©K. Bernstein/Gamma Liaison; p. 27: ©Markel/Gamma Liaison; p. 28: ©John Chiasson/Gamma Liaison; p. 32: ©Burrows/Gamma Liaison; p. 34: AP/Wide World Photos; p. 36–37: AP/Wide World Photos; p. 39: AP/Wide World Photos; p. 40: ©L. Novovitch/Gamma Liaison; p. 41: ©S. Ferry/Gamma Liaison; p. 42: ©Carlos Angel/Gamma Liaison; p. 44: ©Doug Burrows/Gamma Liaison; p. 46: AP/Wide World Photos; p. 48–49: ©John Berry/Gamma Liaison; p. 51: AP/Wide World Photos; p. 54:Gamma Liaison; p. 56: AP/Wide World Photos; p. 59: ©Georges Merillon/Gamma Liaison. Charts and graphs by Sean Kelsey.

Library of Congress Cataloging-in-Publication Data

Salak, John.
    Drugs in Society: are they our suicide pill? / John Salak. — 1st ed.
        p.   cm. — (Issues of our time)
    Includes bibliographical references and index.
    Summary: Describes the history of drug abuse in America, the effects of drug use and abuse, and the current debate surrounding drugs.
    ISBN 0-8050-2572-3 (alk. paper)
    1. Drug abuse—United States—Juvenile literature. 2. Drug abuse—United States—Prevention—Juvenile literature. [1. Drug abuse.] I. Title. II. Series.
HV5809.5.S25   1993
362.29—dc20   93-14105
                                                                                CIP
                                                                                AC

Contents

· · · · ·

1

......

Drug Abuse

When we talk about drug abuse, we are referring to the chronic, or repeated, use of a drug for other than medical reasons. Such use is illegal and does not encompass the use of drugs prescribed by doctors to treat specific diseases or other physical conditions. The illegal use of drugs, or drug abuse, which has reached alarming proportions in the United States, is extremely dangerous. It has serious effects on the physical functioning of the body and on the way people think and act, and it has an impact on society as a whole.

America's drug culture has no ethnic, social, professional, age, gender, or geographic boundaries. It touches everyone—the grade-school

Drugs have invaded every segment of society. Addiction and abuse have become problems for people of all races, ages, professions, and economic backgrounds.

Comedian John Belushi died from a drug overdose. Many famous and talented figures in music and the arts have ruined their lives and careers with drug dependence.

boy and the gray-haired grandmother, the factory worker and the college professor, the jobless individual and the millionaire. And, contrary to popular belief, while drug use is high in America's inner cities, where poverty and social pressures help to encourage abuse, people from the middle and upper class have become the main users. Consider, for example, the many people in prominent positions who have been physically or professionally hurt by their abuse of drugs: comic John Belushi and musician Janis Joplin, both of whom died of drug overdoses; comedian Richard Pryor, who was physically injured while processing cocaine to feed his longtime addiction; Marion Barry, the mayor of Washington, D.C., who was imprisoned for using and purchasing cocaine; and baseball player Steve Howe, who was suspended from the sport because of his drug habit.

The Problem of Drug Abuse

Just how bad is the problem of drug abuse? It is difficult to say precisely because dealing drugs and using them are illegal. Government and social agencies try to measure the impact of drug abuse by looking at various sets of statistics—drug arrests, the number of drug abusers who are hospitalized, and trends in drug-related crimes. But none of these figures gives a complete picture, and many experts claim that statistics are often flawed and misleading anyway. To make measuring the problem more difficult, different studies will frequently report markedly different results. Yet, even with the inability to measure usage accurately, researchers, doctors, and government officials agree that the problem is extensive and likely to get worse in some areas. It is estimated that at least 26 million Americans use drugs at least once a year and that close to 100 million Americans have tried drugs at some time. Within this group, probably 6 million have serious drug problems. And these estimates may be low, according to some experts. The vast majority of drug users are able to function somewhat normally. They can maintain a clean appearance, go to work, and take care of their families. In many cases, however, their drug habit is a time bomb that will ultimately explode.

The size of the U.S. illegal-drug market is staggering, reaching more than $100 billion a year by some estimates. Federal, state, and local officials probably spend about half that amount trying to control the problem. Yet, even these figures pale in comparison to the total cost to the country. Richard Darman, director of the Office of Management and Budget under former president Bush, set the cost at $300 billion a year. That includes funding of antidrug campaigns, treatment, and prevention; and

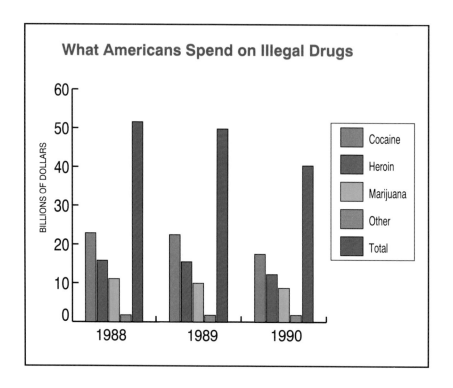

What Americans Spend on Illegal Drugs

the cost of drug-related crime, lost productivity, increased insurance premiums, poorer health, and on-the-job accidents. Ultimately, however, you can't put a price tag on the cost of a single life, or a family, that has been destroyed.

History of Drugs in the World

Drug abuse, of course, is not new to any culture. It is as old as the pyramids—possibly older. What is new is that in the last few decades the problem has grown steadily worse.

Making drugs has become quite a sophisticated business. Admittedly, dozens, if not hundreds, of new illegal drugs are now being developed every year. Yet, even before anyone learned how to refine drugs into the forms we see today, it was realized that certain plants contained powerful chemicals. Where did the first drugs come from? Perhaps 10,000 years ago somebody discovered that it was possible to change the way one felt by drinking the juice of poppy plants, chewing coca leaves, or smoking peyote. Sometimes this was done for medical reasons, such as relieving pain. Often, however, these drugs were used for recreation— to relax or to heighten an individual's physical or mental awareness.

The first documented reference to drugs can be found in the records of the Sumerians of Asia Minor about 7,000 years ago. According to their writings, they discovered a "joy plant"—now believed to be the opium poppy—that was used as a sedative, or calming agent. Records also indicate that in about 3000 B.C. the Chinese were using various plants, including marijuana, for medicinal purposes. Ancient history, in fact, is filled with references to natural remedies and drugs that were believed to help the sick and relieve pain. With increased use, however, came the realization that drugs also had a dangerous side. In about 1500 B.C., the Egyptians left records warning that opium preparations could produce harmful delusions or visions.

The calming effects of the opium poppy have been known to humans for ages. The Sumerians of Asia Minor were among the first to keep records of its use, which goes back more than 7,000 years.

Until the Middle Ages, the people of Asia, South America, and the Middle East seemed much more knowledgeable about drug use and production than the Europeans. It was that knowledge, in fact, that led many European travelers to venture into these relatively unexplored regions to search for drugs to take back to Europe. Many believed that the popular drugs of Asia and South America were magical and powerful and could cure anything.

The Europeans seemed to learn their lessons well. By the middle of the sixteenth century, for example, a Swiss scientist had produced opium in liquid form, which helped to give it more widespread use throughout Europe. While Europeans increasingly embraced opium during the next 200 years, the Chinese remained its biggest consumers. By 1776, the problem was so bad that Chinese rulers created the first recorded antidrug law, making opium smoking punishable by death. That law put China on a collision course with the Europeans. About sixty years later, when China sought to ban opium imports, England and China went to war. By that time, the British controlled the opium trade, and they didn't want to lose this profitable business because of the Chinese import ban. The demand for opium was also soaring outside China—particularly in Europe and North America, where it was used for both medicinal and recreational purposes.

History of Drug Use
in the United States

What is most amazing about America's current drug problem is how little we have learned from the past. Today many people believe that drug addiction is a twentieth-century problem that began about 30 years ago. America, in fact, experienced a serious drug problem more than a century ago. Opium, morphine, and cocaine were the main ingredients in medicines that anyone could purchase openly in many kinds of stores without a doctor's prescription.

Back then it was believed that opium could cure almost anything, and it was commonly available for use with children in such harmless-sounding forms as "Mother Bailey's Quieting Syrup." Science and industry were fast at work during this time developing new drugs that were expected to cure "whatever ailed you." From opium sprang an even stronger drug, morphine, which soon became a common painkiller. Its development coincided with the start of the American Civil War (1861–1865), during which it was widely used to ease the pain of many wounded soldiers. What wasn't known at the time, however, was that morphine was highly addictive. By the war's end, an estimated 400,000 American men were physically and psychologically dependent on morphine, suffering from what became known as the "soldier's disease."

Despite these problems, morphine and other opium-based products became popular recreational drugs. In middle-class circles, for example (where proper behavior was important), it was more acceptable to take a drug than it was to drink alcohol. By 1878, America had a new miracle drug—cocaine. It was developed as an alternative to morphine. Later it was used as a local painkiller for surgery and as a stimulant. Sigmund Freud, the famous Austrian psychiatrist, initially prescribed cocaine for people who were suffering from asthma and stomach problems. Later he backed away from using the drug, admitting that it was harmful. By 1888, cocaine had even found its way into one of America's most popular beverages, Coca-Cola, better known as Coke. It would remain a part of the famous drink's "secret formula" until 1906, when the manufacturer acknowledged the problems of using such a drug and substituted caffeine for cocaine.

While drug use was accepted, the dangerous side effects of opium, morphine, and cocaine didn't go entirely unnoticed. San Francisco enacted the nation's first antidrug law in 1875, when it banned "opium houses,"—homes or rooms where people could go to take opium without being disturbed. The ban didn't work. Yet other cities also tried similar approaches. It wasn't until 35 years later that the federal government banned the smoking of opium.

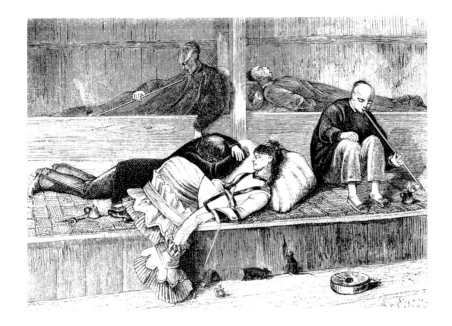

An opium den in San Francisco, around 1880. During the nineteenth century, many powerful drugs were commonly used by the public for recreational purposes.

An international agreement that was designed to control the drug trade also emerged at this time, and a number of federal laws restricting drug use were passed. But the pharmaceutical industry continued to produce new and more powerful drugs—heroin, lysergic acid diethylamide (LSD), phencyclidine (PCP), Demerol, barbiturates (sedatives), and amphetamines (stimulants). While these drugs may have been developed to help people, most of them were used illegally.

Even marijuana, today's most popular illegal substance, was used by doctors for decades to treat patients with coughs and colds and other common health problems. Produced from the leaves and flowers of the hemp plant, which is used in rope products, marijuana was widely and legally grown in the United States well into the twentieth century. As a result, it was not uncommon for both farm workers and wealthy landowners to smoke marijuana, mostly in the form of hashish, one of the most powerful marijuana mixtures. Although the drug was banned by the 1930s, marijuana continued to have widespread use throughout the United States, particularly in the nation's cities.

While drugs have always been a part of American culture, their popularity increased in the 1950s, when writers and social figures started popularizing them. A decade later, in the 1960s, drug use took on a new meaning. It became a way of rebelling, particularly among college students who were disenchanted with America's values and the war in Vietnam, which they viewed as a senseless conflict. Drugs were also being promoted as a way of expanding a person's mind. The popularity that drugs achieved in these two decades paved the way for their dangerous and widespread use in the 1980s.

The 1980s saw the drug industry grow bigger and more deadly—both for users and for dealers. The enormous profits reaped from selling drugs, roughly estimated at $40 billion to $110 billion a year, are one reason for this growth. The emergence of new and relatively cheap drugs has also helped encourage drug use, especially among the urban poor.

Timothy Leary and America's Counterculture

Drug promoters came from all areas of society during the decade of the 1960s. One of the most colorful and controversial prodrug spokespeople was Timothy Leary. Leary was a Harvard University instructor who claimed that psychedelic, or mind-altering, drugs would open up all sorts of "new realities" for those who took them. Soon after trying his first bit of LSD, which is also known as acid, he left Harvard to form the International Foundation of Inner Freedom as a base for promoting a social and intellectual revolution through the use of acid. "During the next few hundred years," Leary once said, "the major activity of man will be the scientific exploration of, and education in, the many universes of awareness that have been opened up by psychedelic drugs."

While not everyone may have understood what Leary was talking about, the use of acid and psychedelic drugs boomed in the 1960s. Aiding this tremendous surge in popularity was the fact that drugs could be easily produced by amateur chemists in virtually any setting. This made it particularly difficult for the police to control their distribution after the drugs became illegal in 1968.

What drew people to LSD or drugs like it? Such drugs seemed to be able to alter reality. Colors could seem brighter, sounds might be more distinct, and objects—either imagined or real—could take on unusual shapes. These effects made mind-altering drugs popular with artists, musicians, and other people who enjoyed the "artist's" life-style. The price the users had to pay for these desired experiences, however, was high. Psychedelic drugs

During the 1960s, Dr. Timothy Leary was one of America's most vocal supporters of LSD and other mind-altering drugs.

are unpredictable and may never completely lose their hold over the user. With many powerful mind-altering drugs, flashbacks and hallucinations (imagined experiences that feel very real) are possible years after someone has stopped taking them. In this way, the effects of these drugs can remain with a person forever.

2

Why People Use Drugs

When one considers the many dangers of drug abuse, it is difficult to imagine that users don't realize the pitfalls. "Why," one asks, "are so many people putting themselves at risk?" Some of the reasons that people use drugs are to ease emotional pain, to experience something new and exciting, to feel more a part of a group, and to fulfill their bodies' demands for the drugs once they have become hooked on them.

Satisfying Emotional Needs and Wants
People in despair, out of work, or troubled by something in their lives often turn to illegal drugs, or alcohol to ease

For many chronic users, drugs offer a way to escape reality and avoid the tough responsibilities of life.

their emotional pain. Drugs also attract thrill seekers. After all, not only do drugs provide a unique physical rush—a sense of power, relaxation, or even visions—but they also allow users to flirt with doing something illegal, something a bit shady. This type of lure is especially enticing because, even though drugs are illegal, they are so abundant that many people believe they'll never get caught using or buying them. Even if they are caught, most casual users mistakenly think they'll get nothing more than a mild warning—but many wind up in jail.

Peer Pressure and Social Acceptance Many people also get drawn into drugs by peer pressure. If they refuse to take drugs, they fear they'll be rejected by their friends. This is especially true for teenagers. What makes peer pressure so forceful is that it is rarely a matter of saying yes or no to drugs. Rather, the pressure occurs in a social setting where the group is involved in taking drugs. The pressure develops because everyone wants to be accepted, and that may mean taking drugs. Often, young people do not fully understand the dangers of drugs. Their primary concern is being accepted.

In certain social or business settings, illegal drugs, such as cocaine or marijuana, are thought to be

acceptable. This is true in many Asian countries, but it is also the case in America, where drugs are common at parties and for business entertaining.

A large crowd of college students enjoys spring break in Fort Lauderdale, Florida. Peer pressure and the need for social acceptance are two of the most influential factors in encouraging drinking and drug use among teens.

The Glamour of Drugs

As noted earlier, America's latest fascination with drugs began in the 1950s. During the 20 years that followed, drugs were championed by writers, musicians, and movie directors who helped introduce them to segments of America that had never seen drugs. This expansion also came at a time when the country was entering a prolonged internal debate about its national values and place in the world. This debate raged at ferocious levels during the 1960s and early 1970s, with riots on college campuses and massive protests against the Vietnam War. Young people were rejecting the past and looking for something new.

Unfortunately, many of these young people discovered marijuana, heroin, and LSD. Added to this was the large-scale drug use among the hundreds of thousands of soldiers in Vietnam. It is estimated that up to 20 percent of the soldiers who returned from Vietnam were chemically dependent.

A decade before, one of the first to popularize drugs, author Jack Kerouac, wrote about his many experiences with drug use. Later, the call to drugs was taken up by many rock musicians such as The Beatles, The Rolling Stones, Jimi Hendrix, Janis Joplin, and Jim Morrison and The Doors, who used their music to promote social causes and counter-culture themes. Even if these celebrities didn't directly promote drugs in their music, they frequently advocated challenging established modes of behavior and pushing for new experiences. Many people took this to mean using drugs. In any event, drugs took their toll on the music industry. Within less than two years, three of rock music's most popular performers, Janis Joplin, Jimi Hendrix, and Jim Morrison would die, victims of drug abuse.

The popular rock band, The Doors, was one of many music groups that glamorized the use of drugs in the 1960s.

In recent years, rock musicians have become increasingly vocal about drug use. Some are opposed to drugs. Their opposition, however, rarely comes in overtly antidrug songs, according to Greg Kot, rock-music critic of the *Chicago Tribune*. Rather, the messages often appear as veiled references. The Red Hot Chili Peppers had great success with the song "Under the Bridge," which refers to the despair of looking for a fix. Other musicians like Tracy Marrow (Ice-T) use their popularity to talk about the consequences of drug abuse through interviews and public-service messages.

On the other hand, some musicians who advocate the use of drugs and who remained silent during the "just-say-no" 1980s are once again singing drugs' praises. In early 1993, for example, a small record company called Re-Hash Records even released an album called "Marijuana's Greatest Hits Revisited."

Many illegal drugs are highly addictive and can cause a powerful psychological and physical dependence in users.

Addiction and Dependence

Once people start using drugs repeatedly—for whatever reason—they develop a strong chemical or emotional addiction, or dependence, and must continue to take them. Even if they want to stop, they can't, because their bodies need the drug. It is a need that occurs even though it is destructive to the body.

Each drug has a different impact on the body, yet all drugs are harmful. Consider cocaine and its offspring, crack (ice). Their immediate effects include dilated pupils and a narrowing of blood vessels. They may also cause an increase in blood pressure, heart rate, breathing rate, and body temperature; a loss of appetite; and sleeping problems. These drugs are initially attractive to users because they provide a sense of exhilaration. But this mood wears off, often leaving the user depressed, and edgy.

In addition to causing physiological problems and addiction, which can last a lifetime, crack and cocaine can lead to death. Even a single dose can cause heart seizures or fatal breathing problems. Moreover, these drugs can result in brain seizures, which can make it difficult for someone to control his or her body. The impact of cocaine and crack on the brain grows the more the drugs are used. This repeated use can create a deadly cycle for chronic abusers.

Easy

Availability Drug abuse has also grown because drugs are now more available, in terms of both quantity and variety. To make matters worse, many of the newer drugs, such as crack, are cheaper and more potent than their predecessors, making their impact and potential harm even greater.

The reason more drugs are available is a matter of simple economics. Illegal drug trafficking has become a big business. In fact, it is a multibillion-dollar business that probably ranks as one of the world's largest. In the United States alone, illegal drug sales are estimated to run between $40 billion and $110 billion a year. This means that Americans are purchasing between $1 billion and $2 billion worth of drugs a week, or between $125 million and $250 million worth of drugs a day.

With billions of dollars involved, the greedy drug pushers are constantly seeking new customers. In addition, the increased demand for drugs has encouraged the formation of illegal drug cartels (combined business groups) in South America and Asia. These organizations are highly sophisticated operations, and as such they have been able to expand their production and distribution networks while they carefully control the street price of their products. By keeping prices affordable for more people, they can, in turn, expand their sales.

The Social Impact of Drugs

The harm that drugs do isn't limited to the user. That's only where it's most obvious. The deadly reach of drugs goes way beyond the user to claim families, friends, and neighborhoods. It can even hurt unborn children. In fact, a 1989 Gallup Poll revealed that 40 percent of Americans have had personal experience with drug abuse either directly or through their friends or community. Beyond this, drug abuse is costly, both in terms of drug prevention programs and the loss of production in industry. Ultimately, there is no way to escape the impact of drug abuse, even if you're not a user and you don't know anyone who takes drugs. The influence of drugs is everywhere, and everyone in society bears the cost.

In recent decades, drug-related deaths and violence have increased dramatically, as heavily armed street gangs have taken control of drug trafficking.

Family

Problems Drug abuse is both a financial burden to families and a disruptive element in their lives. Drug habits can cost hundreds of dollars a week. To support a habit, parents or children will rob money from their families.

In addition, the demand to meet an addiction can be so great that users commit crimes to get money. Not only does a drug habit destroy the mind and body, but it may also lead to imprisonment. Either way, the children of drug abusers are left without the kind of help and support that their parents should be providing for them. Even after users serve jail time, their criminal records can haunt them for the rest of their lives. Finding a job can be difficult for people with criminal records, and children of these people may be deprived of life's basic needs.

This type of pressure—physical breakdown, demands for money, and possible legal problems—threatens to break traditional family bonds. From 1987 to 1990, for example, foster-care placement of children in neighborhoods hit hard by the crack epidemic rose by almost a third.

Crack

Babies Before they even have the opportunity to become a part of society, some children are hurt by drugs. Pregnant women, in addition to putting

Marion Barry: A Career and a Marriage Destroyed

Marion S. Barry, Jr., an African American, rose through local political offices to become the mayor of the city of Washington, D.C. As head of the nation's capital, he was a symbol of hope to other African Americans and minorities. Unfortunately, his involvement with drugs destroyed both his career and his marriage, cost him his freedom, and disillusioned those who had looked up to him as a role model.

Barry had been both an alcoholic and a drug user for many years before entering politics and becoming mayor. He continued this destructive life-style even after assuming office. In 1990, his secret past finally caught up with him, when a government sting operation videotaped the mayor in a hotel room while he was smoking crack.

A grand jury followed up by charging Barry with 11 drug-related counts in addition to 3 charges of perjury (lying under oath). He was eventually cleared on all but 1 of these charges. Although he was found innocent on many counts, he was convicted of cocaine possession. During the celebrated trial, witnesses and even his own lawyer admitted that Barry was a drug user. In the end, Barry resigned his office and was sentenced to six months in jail. Effi, his wife of more than 10 years, stood by Barry through the difficult trial but later sought a divorce.

Besides the many famous drug-addicted figures, like Marion Barry, there are millions of chronic abusers and addicts from every walk of life who have lost control over their lives because of drugs like cocaine, crack, and heroin. The federal government estimates there are at least 6 million Americans who are currently drug dependent in one way or another. Some experts think this is a conservative estimate and place the figure much higher. The numbers, no matter what the discrepancy, clearly indicate that a significant portion of the American population is battling the tough problems of drug dependence.

While he was the mayor of Washington, D.C., Marion S. Barry, Jr., was arrested for illegal drug use and possession.

themselves at risk by abusing drugs, put their unborn children at risk. During pregnancy, chronic drug use can cause serious problems, including miscarriage, premature labor or delivery, and internal bleeding that can kill both the mother and the child.

With the introduction of crack, the problem of drug abuse during pregnancy has taken on national proportions. The babies of women who are crack users are born addicted to the drug. Approximately 100 thousand of these crack babies, as they are called, are born each year. Crack babies are more likely to have medical problems than normal babies. They are at increased risk of suffering a heart attack right after birth, and they may have a dangerously low birth weight, improperly formed genitals and kidneys, a smaller-than-normal head, slow reflexes, and an increased chance of developing seizures, which can lead to crib death. Moreover, studies are now starting to reveal that crack babies may have learning problems later in life.

Each year, thousands of babies are born to drug-addicted mothers in the United States. At special centers, like Hale House in New York City, some of these children receive the proper care and attention they cannot get from their mothers.

Youthful

Corruption One of the greatest tragedies of the drug trade is that in an attempt to open up new markets to sell drugs, dealers are pursuing younger customers.

A 1990 study by the Rand Corporation on the impact of drugs on low-income communities found, for example, that about 15 percent of the ninth and tenth graders whom the study had interviewed dealt with drugs as dealers, messengers, or lookouts. Of this group, fewer than one third used drugs themselves. In 1992, the National Parents' Resource Institute for Drug Education study reported that the use of drugs among junior and senior high school students appeared to be rising for the first time in several years. And in early 1993, the results of a survey conducted at the University of Michigan reported a rise in the use of marijuana, cocaine, and LSD by eighth graders. This trend was also independently noted by specialists in treatment centers across the nation.

Drug abuse robs young people of a normal and productive life and can often interfere with the learning process and their ability to work effectively with others. It also tends to make young people violent, and it puts them at risk of contracting AIDS through the use of shared needles. They risk dying as the result of a drug overdose.

A Family Torn Apart by Drugs

The story of Alexander Warner (not his real name) is a perfect example of the destructive nature of drugs on an entire family—on Alexander, on his sister, on his baby brother, and on his mother and father.

Alexander began taking drugs when he was 11 years old. Three years later, he introduced his 12-year-old sister, Cathy, to drugs. Together, Alexander and Cathy then proceeded to get their 2-year-old brother, Chris, high by blowing marijuana in his face. Cathy and her friends even got the family parakeet high, putting pot seeds in his bird feed and blowing marijuana into his cage—just to watch his wacky behavior!

Pam and Jim Warner caught on to the fact that their son Alexander was on drugs, but they had no idea that Cathy and Chris were also involved. They constantly argued over how to handle the situation. Jim wanted to be his son's pal, while Pam wanted to take immediate action. Pam had to make a decision on her own. She sent Alexander to a hospital that had a special drug-treatment program for children.

Once he was released from the hospital, Alexander went right back on drugs. Lacking the support of her husband, Pam started to rely on Cathy for advice, unaware, at that point, that her daughter was doing pot, hash, speed, quaaludes, cocaine, acid, PCP, nitrous oxide, and prescription drugs. Again beside herself and unable to cope, Pam threw Alexander out of the house.

After Jim took Alexander back one snowy night, Pam walked out. While living in a motel room, she became ill and almost lost the baby she was carrying. After recuperating, and before leaving her family for a second time, Pam returned home to this nightmare:

"...{Alexander} started to threaten me again. And {Chris} couldn't be left alone anytime even in his own room. He would be sitting just calmly watching television, then he'd just jump up and start yelling. He would run into his room and get under the bed. He kept crying, 'They always yell at me....' I didn't find out until later that {Alexander} and {Cathy} had been taking him downstairs and getting him high. He was scared to death of them. That's when I decided...to leave.... I resented it a lot because I felt like my husband chose two druggie kids over me."

Cathy's life got even more messed up when her mother left. All she could focus on was how to get high. This is how Cathy described those difficult times:

"I had a lot of different boyfriends.... I tried to get the ones who were dealing.... I just used them to get drugs. It didn't make any difference if I liked them...just so they had drugs.

"I was hitchhiking one time and this guy stopped to pick me up. He was about twenty-four. And he asked me if I wanted to go to a motel and get high. He had hash. So I went to the motel with him. We got high, and I went to bed with him."

This may seem like an unusual story, but it's not. According to Dr. Miller Newton, who worked with the Warner family and has counseled many other drug-abusing children and their families, the Warner family "is not so different from the hundreds, indeed thousands, of drug-torn families in America."

Many students are very much aware of the problems that can be caused by drug abuse. According to a survey of teenagers conducted by the National Institute on Drug Abuse, the problem of drug abuse is the primary concern of teens, ranking above their concern about the environment, education, the homeless, and AIDS.

Violence Violence has also become an almost inseparable part of the drug culture, affecting both individuals and communities. In scrambling to get money to buy drugs, users often commit crimes, alarming residents of a neighborhood. Adding to this threat is the violence that erupts among rival drug dealers.

Crack abuse presents a classic example of the relationship between drugs and crime. In the first part of the 1980s, before crack emerged on the drug scene, violent crime in America was decreasing. In the roughly five years after the inexpensive and easily available drug appeared, the crime rate soared. Aggravated assaults rose by a third, while robberies jumped by 15 percent. During the 1980s, drug-related arrests tripled, which then led to the doubling of the nation's prison population. Drugs seem to be part of the criminal culture in general. By the end of the 1980s, at least half of those arrested in the nation's major cities had used crack or cocaine.

Gangs and the Drug Trade

The growth of inner-city gangs has gone hand in hand with the rising violence associated with drug trafficking. Gangs no longer battle over turf just for the sake of their territory. They fight because controlling a neighborhood usually means controlling the drug trade in that neighborhood. And that means money. The profits from dealing drugs have also allowed gangs to purchase sophisticated automatic weapons, which make them even more dangerous.

The connection of gangs to the drug trade has grown as gang membership has soared in the last decade. Contrary to popular movie images, gangs are not just groups of teenagers who live in a particular neighborhood. Gangs have gone national. The Crips and Bloods, two Los Angeles–based gangs, may have as many as 50,000 members in more than 30 states and 100 cities. Experts estimate gangs may control one third of the U.S. crack trade.

The crack trade has also helped other gangs spread their influence. For example, Jamaican gangs, known as posses, have taken a large share of the crack business in East Coast cities. The Bureau of Alcohol, Tobacco and Firearms estimates that these posses control another third of America's crack trade.

Drug-related violence has increased as street gangs have taken over more control of drug distribution.

Drugs in
the Workplace
Drug abuse not only claims users, their families, and neighborhoods, but it also costs American industry a great deal of money. It is estimated that in terms of lost production, absenteeism, accidents, medical claims, and thefts, the drug epidemic costs the United States $60 billion a year. Large companies such as General Motors and Motorola may lose up to $1 billion a year in drug-related expenses.

In recent years, companies have started to fight back. Most major companies have established employee-assistance programs (EAPs) designed to provide counseling and treatment to employees seeking help for alcohol or drug abuse. Helping an employee who may quit or be fired because of a drug problem is good for business. As many companies note, investing in EAPs saves money in the long run because businesses cut expenditures on hiring and training new workers.

Other companies give job applicants drug tests before hiring them. Through sophisticated chemical studies, these tests are able to tell whether a person has used any number of drugs in recent days. About two thirds of the largest companies—those with at least 5,000 workers—run these tests.

In many cases, drug testing is not just a matter of saving a company money, but also a case of saving lives. A New York City subway crash in 1991 that killed 5 and hurt 170 underscored the point when a crack vial was found in the train engineer's cab. This incident, and others like it, have led many organizations to conduct periodic testing to ensure that workers in safety-sensitive positions, such as bus drivers, train conductors, airplane pilots, and air-traffic controllers, are drug-free. A 1989 Gallup Poll reported that a significant majority of employees supported drug testing for themselves, and 90 percent thought that drug testing was appropriate for anyone involved in a safety-sensitive job.

In 1991, an engineer high on crack caused a subway crash in New York City that killed 5 people and injured 170. Tragic incidents that result from drugs in the workplace have become more common in recent years.

One of the many notions about drug abuse is that addicts are all destitute outcasts of society who really don't try to fit in. This, however, is not the case. Of the 26 million people estimated to take drugs at least once a year, two thirds of them, or about 16 million, hold regular jobs. When they are combined with those who are

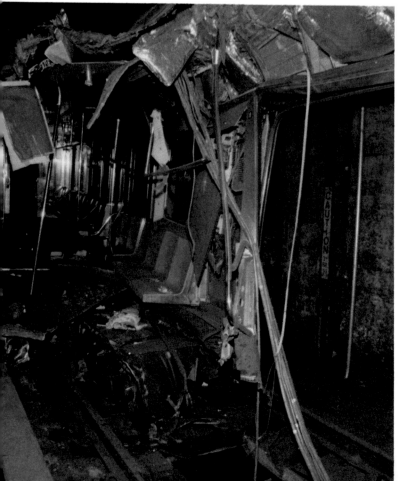

dependent on alcohol, health officials estimate that about 10 percent of the nation's work force is addicted to drugs or alcohol.

Drugs
and AIDS
Perhaps one of the most tragic impacts of drugs on society has been the AIDS epidemic, which has gripped both the nation and the world in recent years. While AIDS is not a direct result of drug abuse, the disease can be spread by AIDS-infected drug users who share needles with others.

New Haven, Connecticut, responded to this problem in 1990 with an experimental needle-exchange program that set off a national debate. The aim of the program was to give drug users clean needles every week in hopes of preventing the spread of AIDS. Critics claimed that the program would encourage drug use. Even the federal government criticized the plan. Yet, the New Haven experiment had some positive results. According to some Yale University researchers, the rate of AIDS cases has dropped by 33 percent, and the percentage of returned needles testing positive for the AIDS virus has gone from 68 to 41 percent. Encouraged by these results, other cities, such as New York and San Francisco, have established needle-exchange programs. Such programs, however, still remain illegal in most U.S. cities.

4

....

The War on Drugs

What's America's longest war? It is not the American Revolution, World War II, or even the Vietnam War. It is the country's war on drugs. America formally declared war on drugs more than 20 years ago, but it has actually been battling increasing drug consumption for more than a century. The fight has been a costly one in terms of both the number of lives lost and the amount of money spent. Today federal and state governments spend tens of billions of dollars each year on everything from fighting small-time street pushers to arranging sophisticated international agreements designed to block the flow of drugs into the country.

U.S. Customs agents load bales of marijuana onto a truck in New York after seizing eight tons of the drug at Brooklyn's Pier 10. Tens of billions of dollars are spent each year in America in an effort to stem the flow of drugs.

Federal

Legislation
Since the first antidrug law was enacted in 1875, the federal government has been increasingly involved in controlling drug abuse and drug sales. In fact, by 1970 a total of 55 federal laws had been put into place either restricting or prohibiting drug use. The rise in consumption during the 1960s spurred even more federal action, as drug abuse went from a problem to a national crisis of epidemic proportions.

President Richard Nixon responded by declaring a "war on drugs." In 1970, Nixon's declaration led to the federal laws on drugs being put under a unified code called the Controlled Substances Act. A national commission was established to investigate the causes and possible solutions to the problem of growing drug use. It recommended, among other things, that marijuana be decriminalized and that a single federal agency be formed to oversee the government's antidrug efforts.

The government stepped up its fight in 1984 with the creation of the Omnibus Drug Bill—a series of programs and strict policies designed to halt the spread of drugs in America. Not long afterward, there were some indications that overall drug use had decreased. Unfortunately, there were also signs of new problems on the horizon. If drug use is actually declining, at least in some segments of the population, it is the result of many factors. Tough economic times, for example, have certainly helped curtail drug use among casual users, who find drugs too expensive to buy. Even the violence related to drugs, particularly crack, has had its benefits. It has helped to raise public concern and stimulate action.

Federal Expenditures

There are many different ways to fight a war. Mostly, however, a war is fought with money. In the 10 years from 1983 to 1993, federal expenditures for drug control rose from less than $2 billion a year to more than $12 billion. That's a fivefold increase. During roughly the same period, 1981 to 1991, federal, state, and local antidrug spending totalled more than $100 billion. In 1992 alone, the United States is estimated to have spent a total of $40 billion to control drug abuse.

Federal money is spent in three areas: treatment and prevention, international drug controls, and domestic (national) law enforcement. Under the Reagan and Bush administrations, new emphasis was placed on enforcing antidrug laws—at the expense of treating addicts and preventing young people from becoming involved with drugs.

President Clinton's 1993 budget reflected this same emphasis. However, since the budget was due

President Richard Nixon was the first to formally declare a "war on drugs" in 1970. Since that time, the drug epidemic has grown steadily, faster than any efforts to stop it.

Blocking illegal drugs from entering the United States is one of the primary focuses of federal anti-drug programs. Here, U.S. Coast Guard members unload a 9,000-pound shipment of cocaine that they intercepted.

before Clinton chose his drug-program head, and since Janet Reno, the new attorney general, has a prodrug-treatment record, many think that more money will be included for treatment programs.

Typically, about 25 to 30 percent of federal spending is put into prevention and reducing demand, compared with about 45 percent that goes toward domestic enforcement. A substantial amount also goes into efforts to block drugs from getting into the United States. This is done in part by helping foreign governments reduce production in their own countries and thereby slashing the flow of drugs into the United States. Of the $12.7 billion spent in 1992, $3 billion—27 percent—went to fund these international programs.

International Involvement
America consumes more drugs than it produces. Whatever it doesn't produce, it gets from other countries. Drugs usually come into this country in a raw or pure form. Once here, drug traffickers take these drugs and process them before

distributing them on the streets. Processing can include any number of steps. It might involve diluting or cutting the drug to reduce its strength. One example is cocaine. It comes into this country in a pure powder form and is mixed with other drugs or substances before it is sold. This mixing not only reduces its strength, but it also increases the profit margins for the sellers because they are

Panama, Noriega, and a Real War

The war on drugs took on a new meaning in December 1989, when the United States invaded Panama after a long-standing dispute with Manuel Noriega, the country's president.

In the mid-1980s, it became evident that Noriega was using his position to sell drugs in the United States. This led to various indictments against him for drug-related crimes. For many years, federal officials tried unsuccessfully to bring Noriega to the United States to stand trial. As the United States increased its pressure, Noriega mocked America's inability to get him. During the 1989 U.S. invasion of Panama, Noriega was captured, brought to trial, convicted, and imprisoned in the United States. At the same time, federal officials helped establish a new Panamanian government that they hoped would take a hard stance against local drug running.

The cost of capturing Noriega was high. Twenty-three U.S. soldiers died during the invasion, and 300 others were wounded. The toll was even greater for the Panamanians, who lost 600 people. The fighting, while brief, also disrupted Panama's economy, causing more than $2 billion in damages.

In December 1989, U.S. troops invaded Panama and captured Manuel Noriega, the country's president.

able to stretch out their expensive main ingredient—cocaine. Sometimes drugs are further refined or actually turned into a secondary drug, as is the case with opium, which can be turned into heroin. In recent years, crack, a mixture of cocaine, baking soda, and water, has also appeared on the drug scene. Since it is much cheaper than cocaine and provides a more intense high, it is much more widely used than cocaine.

While drug-processing plants exist in the United States, many of America's most popular drugs—heroin, cocaine, marijuana—come into the country from overseas. To stop this illegal trade, the United States has become involved in international efforts with the governments of the major South American producers—Peru, Bolivia, and Colombia. International efforts can run from sharing information to training foreign police forces to actually using U.S. troops in conjunction with local soldiers to battle drug dealers.

One of the latest efforts involves Peru, which produces about 70 percent of the world's cocaine. The plan calls for the United States

Because most of the illegal drugs that plague the United States are grown and processed in Central and South America, federal antidrug programs have tried to organize efforts to destroy production facilities at their origin. Here, the Colombian police spray opium poppies with a poison that will destroy the crop.

to feed, equip, train, outfit, and adequately pay the police and armed forces who will be fighting drug traffickers and those who support them. As part of the effort, the United States provides military equipment and training to help Peruvian government forces battle drug dealers and the forces of Shining Path, a rebel group that is working with drug dealers in their effort to overthrow the government. Once trained, the Peruvian forces will attack traffickers by seizing their buildings and assets and destroying their production and transportation centers at their source.

Private and Public Efforts Not only the federal government but also local groups and social organizations have responded to the war on drugs. One of the most ambitious programs that is designed to combat drug abuse comes from Drug Free America, a private, not-for-profit group. Formed in 1987, Drug Free America has raised more than $1 billion dollars for a massive advertising campaign that has changed the way antidrug messages are developed. The group uses television, radio, and the print medium to present tough and often graphic ads that attack crack, cocaine, and marijuana. By 1991, the organization had aired 8,600 television commercials along with thousands of print and radio ads.

Violent crime and other social problems have motivated many urban communities to organize against drug gangs and illegal activities that threaten the safety of families and children.

Schools are also deeply involved in battling drugs. Sometimes schools are directly involved in drug problems, but they also work with outside agencies. One program developed in the late 1970s has been particularly effective at helping young people cope. Life Skills Training (LST) works in schools to teach students how to handle all sorts of situations, solve problems, and feel more confident through a 15-session course centered on developing positive group skills. Studies have found that alcohol and marijuana use among those completing the course is 50 to 75 percent lower than among non-participating students.

STAR (Student Taught Awareness and Resistance) is another program designed to help young people stay away from drugs and build positive attitudes toward working in groups. The focus of STAR, most of whose programs are in Kansas, Missouri, and Washington, D.C., high schools, is to have students work closely with their parents so they can learn to discuss problems that might lead to drug use. As part of the program, community leaders and support agencies also join in to create activities, such as athletics, which give students an alternative to drugs. As with the LST program, students who are involved in STAR tested significantly lower in drug use than students outside the program.

Both programs, which are usually available to students up through their years of high school, are generally part of the school curriculum. Some schools, however, don't have the money to commit to programs like these. Often they turn to DARE

Bridgeport's Sweat Team

In Bridgeport, Connecticut, a middle-sized industrial city that was seriously hurt by the economic problems of the early 1990s, city officials, nonprofit social agencies, and the local police have teamed up to create jobs and recreational activities for students to keep them off the streets and away from drugs.

One of the more unusual efforts in this plan is the Sweat Team (Students Who Entertain Artistic Thought). The program allows about two dozen students, paid with money from antidrug grants, to create activities for other youths. Their efforts resulted in the organization of tennis classes, dances, picnics, block parties, festivals, an inner-city basketball league for youths, and softball games.

In addition to planning activities, Sweat Team members deliver constant antidrug messages. And the police help out, too. Not only do they work with the students at developing programs, but they also help them to present more effective antidrug messages.

(Drug Abuse Resistance Education), which is a learning and sensitivity-based antidrug program that is offered nationally to about 5 million fifth and sixth graders through local police departments. While studies indicate that DARE is not as successful as programs like LST or STAR, it does build better relations between local police and students.

The Problems of
Fighting the War
It is difficult to gauge whether the United States is making any headway in fighting drugs because the problem is both large and diverse. There are millions of users, and they deal in hundreds of different types of drugs. Also, new drugs are being created all the time, and each drug presents the police with a new set of problems. Each drug, for example, has different production and distribution systems. Cocaine comes from South America; marijuana comes from Mexico, Colombia, and the United States; and heroin comes from Asia. And a little goes a long way. Twenty square miles of opium poppies can supply enough heroin to meet U.S. annual demand. And the nation's annual cocaine consumption could be brought into the country by four 747 cargo planes. Moreover, drugs such as ice and LSD, can be made in someone's basement. It is almost as though the police are trying to hold back the tide with a bucket.

Pablo Escobar and the Medellín Cartel

International drug trafficking is not just a multibillion-dollar business, but it is also a very powerful political force. In some cases, the grip of drug dealers can virtually paralyze a country. Nothing underscores this power more than the story of Pablo Escobar and Colombia's Medellín cartel. Named for a town in Colombia, the cartel headed by Escobar is reputed to be the world's largest crime organization. By the late 1980s, the Medellín cartel was exporting between 300 and 400 metric tons of cocaine annually and was responsible for about 80 percent of the cocaine and crack sold on America's streets. The group's annual revenues reached about $4 billion to $5 billion.

Pablo Escobar

Obviously, this type of business demands a highly efficient and sophisticated operation that involves widespread production centers, complex distribution networks, detailed financial dealings, and a centralized administration. Yet, today's drug operations also need to rely on strong-armed tactics and fear to survive. Under Escobar's guidance, the Medellín cartel excelled at crushing all kinds of opposition. It used terrorism, murder, and bribery to control and manipulate politicians, police and government forces, the general population, rival drug dealers, and even Escobar's own men. It was a policy of control that resulted in numerous deaths.

During the 1980s alone, the cartel was directly responsible for the murder of 50 Colombian judges, 170 judicial employees, a presidential candidate, two ministers of justice, the head of the National Police Anti-Narcotics Bureau, an attorney general, a dozen journalists, and more than 400 people in the military and on police forces. The cartel also tried to pay off Colombia's $15 billion foreign debt as a means of buying protection from the government. As head of this cartel, Escobar often seemed above the law. Even during his 1991–1992 imprisonment, he gained the right to pick his guards and was thus able to run his massive drug network from his cell.

Once Escobar escaped from jail, he set off a reign of terror. Through his associates, he reportedly placed about 50 car bombs that killed and wounded hundreds. In addition, his cartel set up a bounty of $2,100 for every police officer killed. As a result, local hitmen murdered more than 100 officers in about six months. The violence, however, escalated even beyond Escobar's control. In an attempt to stop Escobar, government forces and local police persisted in their efforts to crush the cartel, which led to the capture or surrender of many of Escobar's top aides. In addition, a number of former associates have personally declared war on Escobar. Called the *Pepes*, which stands for People Persecuted by Pablo Escobar, they have killed and kidnapped dozens of Escobar's supporters, taking the law into their own hands. Their efforts, along with those of the police, have driven Escobar deep into hiding.

5

Where We Stand

There is no clear-cut picture as to how much progress is being made in the war on drugs. In the 1980s, there were reports that drug use had declined overall and specifically among certain segments of the population. There were also reports that interest had been renewed in some of the more popular drugs of the 1960s. Some people labeled the information in these reports misleading. Against this backdrop, the debate continues on what is to be done to battle drugs in the 1990s. Do we toughen penalties? Increase treatment? Legalize drugs? There are no simple answers. There is only the enormous challenge to keep fighting.

Elementary-school children listen to an antidrug talk given by a U.S. Customs agent. Educating young people about the dangers of drugs is one of the best ways to control the growth of the problem.

A Look at
the Recent Past

As the 1980s wore on and the 1990s began, drug abuse, according to some reports, was on the decline. Bob Martinez, director of the White House Office of National Drug Control Policy under President Bush, reported that overall drug consumption had fallen by almost 60 percent from 1979 to 1991. The decline was even sharper among young people, he added. From 1985 to 1991, drug use among this group fell by 79 percent. Cocaine consumption was particularly affected, declining by 67 percent. The popular drugs of the 1960s and 1970s—heroin, LSD, and speed—had also faded from view. Most of the progress of the late 1980s was made among America's middle class. The government, however, could not make inroads into drug abuse in the inner cities.

Interpreting
the Numbers

Measuring drug abuse is not easy. No matter how many reports are used, no one knows the exact number of people affected by drugs or the quantity of drugs that find their way into the country. Regardless of who's counting, the numbers basically reflect an educated guess.

Officials from the Drug Policy Foundation in Washington, D.C., for example, were quick to attack Martinez's reports on drug abuse. While they admitted that drug consumption had declined since 1979, they felt that the government's reports on the improvements were misleading. The foundation claimed that crack use had not really declined under President Bush, that cocaine imports had actually increased every year under his administration, and that drug-treatment programs had been neglected.

Others warned against attaching too much weight to any figures. Even if reports aren't misleading, they pointed out, drug patterns change too quickly for snapshot reports to provide deep insights.

In 1990, for example, President Bush reported that crack and cocaine consumption were finally declining. He also announced a 4 percent drop in those with serious drug problems and a decline among casual users, especially young people.

In that same year, a study by the University of Michigan supported his findings, noting that only one third of high school students had tried an illegal drug during the previous year. In the late 1970s, similar studies found that more than half of high school students had taken a drug at least once during the previous 12 months.

Another study by the University of California in Berkeley also found that drug tolerance appeared to be waning. Only 24 percent of a recent freshman class supported legalizing marijuana compared with 60 percent who had backed it 20 years earlier.

Bob Martinez was appointed America's drug czar by President Bush. As the director of the White House Office of National Drug Control Policy, Martinez was involved for many years in exploring various options for fighting drugs.

Even the Bush administration's efforts to curb the foreign drug problem appeared to be making some progress by 1990—for the first time in decades, worldwide coca-plant production had declined slightly.

The 1990s:
New Problems, Old Drugs
By 1992, new reports were claiming that use of cocaine and marijuana were on the rise. Most of the increases were coming among inner-city youths and longtime users. Even Bob Martinez admitted that drugs in the inner cities remained a problem. The rise in drug-related emergency-room visits underscored the

Drug Use Among America's High School Students
(percent of those who have used)

Class of	1975	1980	1984	1985	1986	1987	1988	1989	1990	1991
Marijuana/Hashish	47.3	60.3	54.9	54.2	50.9	50.2	47.2	43.7	40.7	36.7
Inhalants	NA	11.9	14.4	15.4	15.9	17.0	16.7	17.6	18.0	17.6
Hallucinogens	16.3	13.3	10.7	10.3	9.7	10.3	8.9	9.4	9.4	9.6
LSD	11.3	9.3	8.0	7.5	7.2	8.4	7.7	8.3	8.7	8.8
PCP	NA	9.6	5.0	4.9	4.8	3.0	2.9	3.9	2.8	2.9
Cocaine	9.0	15.7	15.1	17.3	17.0	15.2	12.2	10.3	9.4	7.8
Crack	NA	NA	NA	NA	NA	5.6	4.8	4.7	3.5	3.1
Heroin	2.2	1.1	1.3	1.2	1.1	1.2	1.1	1.3	1.3	0.9
Stimulants	NA	NA	27.9	26.2	23.4	21.6	19.8	19.1	17.5	15.4
Sedatives (3)	18.2	14.9	13.3	11.8	10.4	8.7	7.8	7.4	5.3	6.7
Barbiturates (3)	16.9	11.0	9.9	9.2	8.4	7.4	6.7	6.5	6.8	6.2
Alcohol	90.4	93.2	92.6	92.2	91.3	92.2	92.0	90.7	89.5	88.0
Cigarettes	73.6	71.0	69.7	68.8	67.6	67.2	66.4	65.7	64.4	63.1

NA=Not Available

(3) Only drug use that was not under a doctor's orders.

Source: National Institute on Drug Abuse/Univ. of Michigan Inst. for Social Research

trend. In the first few years of the 1990s they rose steadily in the major inner cities, even though they declined in the suburbs.

Even more alarming were the numerous reports in 1991 and 1992 that consumption of heroin and acid was increasing. In the case of heroin, the jump was attributed to economics. The production of opium poppy, from which heroin is made, began to soar in the late 1980s. This led to a sharp reduction in the street price of a heroin fix. After holding at about $10 for years, the overproduction and an effort to find more customers had driven the price down to about $6 a bag. This cheap dope had attracted new consumers. Heroin dealers also took a lesson from their crack counterparts and created a smokable form of heroin that is even more marketable. The result: deaths from heroin began rising, as did the number of addicts.

Police are reporting that LSD and other hallucinogens are also making a comeback. While experts claim it is unlikely that these drugs will ever be as popular as cocaine was during the 1980s, their reemergence suggests a new cycle of addiction.

Approaches to Drug Control

The debate over drug abuse isn't limited to how many people are involved or how much money drug dealers make. There is also a

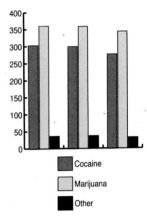

What High School Students Spent on Drugs, 1991
(in millions of dollars)

Cocaine
Marijuana
Other

Source: "What America's Users Spend on Illegal Drugs," art Office of National Drug Control Policy Technical Paper, June 1991.

Many people believe that increasing police forces and toughening prison sentences for drug-related crimes are among the best approaches to the nation's drug problem.

controversy over how to stop drug abuse. There are four main approaches. The first is to create and enforce laws that prevent the sale and consumption of drugs. Another option is to work to discourage young people from ever using drugs. There are also those who believe that the greatest emphasis should be placed on treating addicts in order to get them off drugs. Finally, many advocate that the most effective way to control consumption is to legalize drugs, or at least some drugs, such as marijuana. This would remove organized crime from the business; generate millions, or perhaps billions, of dollars in tax revenues that could be put into education; and allow the government to control and regulate drug distribution centers.

Evaluating
the Efforts
It is unlikely that any one approach to the problem of drug abuse in the United States will be adopted completely. What is clear is that federal, state, and local governments, along with churches, schools, and civic organizations, are expected to continue pouring billions of dollars into fighting drugs along a broad front.

It isn't a matter of whether drugs can be eliminated but whether the problem can be controlled and what the best approach or approaches are to control the problem.

International agreements to stop the flow of drugs represent a temporary measure at best, and the government's efforts in this area have not been given a very high mark. The General Accounting Office (GAO), a federal agency that analyzes government spending, claims that while the Pentagon has directed a lot of military resources into stopping the flow of drugs, it hasn't worked well with other government and civilian groups. According to the GAO, success will come only when all these groups work together effectively and develop new technologies that will allow them to examine millions of air and ship cargo containers that arrive from South America and are often used to hide drug shipments.

Even the government admits it is having problems. Federal-law-enforcement officials estimate that 70 to 90 percent of the cocaine shipped to the United States gets past them.

Mathea Falco, former assistant secretary of state for international narcotics matters and member of the national Drug Abuse Council, has been involved with fighting drugs at many levels inside government and in the private sector for years. She warns that the country's war on drugs may be misdirected. In her book *The Making of a Drug-Free America*, she comments: "What we need is not more money, but an entirely different strategy, one that puts into practice what we have learned in recent years about reducing the demand for drugs. Many of the most promising new approaches are not expensive compared to the costs of prison construction and sophisticated high-tech equipment intended to seal the nation's borders against the drug traffic."

President Clinton's Proposals

During his campaign for the presidency, Bill Clinton began formalizing his ideas on drug control. Now that he is president, he is studying the issue further and has developed a multipoint plan to attack abuse that goes beyond many of the traditional schemes. Some of the ideas for his antidrug campaign tie in with his anticrime strategies, which include adding 100,000 patrol officers nationwide and supporting the death penalty to control crime.

While these measures have yet to be put into practice, Clinton has proposed setting up a national police corps staffed with military veterans and active military personnel. He also wants to create boot camps for nonviolent first-time offenders that would help them develop both discipline and self-esteem. The boot-camp idea has already been tried out with some juvenile delinquents with a high degree of success. Fewer than a third of the delinquents who have gone to boot camps have returned to crime. On the other hand, of those delinquents

As president, Bill Clinton outlined a number of anti-drug approaches that he supported. Among them are increasing addict treatment facilities, enforcing the death penalty for serious crimes, and creating strict, army-like camps for nonviolent first-time offenders in order to discourage further crime in the future.

who have been sent to jail, more than one half have returned to a life of crime.

Clinton also wants to provide drug treatment on demand, increase funding for drug education, and develop programs to encourage those living in public housing to organize themselves to help rid their neighborhoods of drug dealers. The president asked former New York police commissioner Lee J. Brown to be the drug czar, a position that Clinton elevated to the rank of a cabinet post. Brown will head the Office of National Drug Control Policy to work on programs to coordinate the country's war on drugs.

Legalizing
Drugs Perhaps the most controversial approach to the country's drug problem is the legalization of drugs, which is supported by a small but vocal number of people from all political backgrounds. Some supporters argue that no one has the right to tell another person what to do with his or her body, even if it is harmful. They also argue that as long as people want to take drugs, there is no way the government can stop them. Drug users, they say, will always find a way to get drugs. One group, the National Organization for the Reform of Marijuana Laws (NORML), has worked for years to legalize marijuana and has been successful in getting some states to decriminalize possession of small amounts.

Some supporters of drug legalization also argue that legalizing drugs may actually decrease usage. According to them, it will take drug trafficking away from the criminals, reducing the risk of violence. The price of drugs would also drop, probably reducing the need to rob to support a drug habit. Moreover, the billions of federal and state dollars that presently go into enforcing drug laws could go into prevention and treatment, instead.

In many European countries—the Netherlands, Switzerland, and Great Britain, for example—the government's approach to dealing with addicts is different than in America. The strategy in these countries is to attack the dealer and treat the user. As a result, governments try to control drug use so that the addicts feel they can have access to government-sponsored programs to receive help.

The Netherlands is probably the leading example. While sales of heroin, cocaine, and marijuana carry heavy fines and prison terms of up to 12 years, holding these drugs for personal use only carries a penalty of up to 1 year. In certain "tolerance zones," however, these laws are relaxed. For example, Dutch authorities permit coffee shops to sell marijuana even though it is against the law, but they strictly enforce laws against their selling cocaine and heroin. They also allow drug use and sales in certain parts of the city, although they monitor these areas very closely to curb street crime. By handling the problem in this way, Dutch authorities hope that addicts will not totally drift away from society and put themselves beyond help. Their efforts appear to be paying off, as the drug use has dropped slightly in the Netherlands since the mid-1980s. In fact, the Dutch boast one of the lowest levels of drug abuse in Western Europe.

While the Dutch experiment has worked, a similar one in Zurich, Switzerland, has not. In 1989, city officials created a "tolerance zone" for illegal drug use in Platzspitz Park. By doing this, Swiss officials hoped to provide better medical and social services to drug users and at the same time control street crime. The effort, however, backfired. The park attracted thousands of drug users, which overwhelmed the local services and created many more problems than it solved. The park became a danger-

A marijuana "menu" is displayed on a table in a Dutch coffee shop. In the Netherlands and other European countries, where the approach to the drug problem is different than in America, there have been some positive results, including a reduced rate of drug abuse and less drug-related violent crime.

ous and deteriorating jungle that raised a storm of protest from city residents. Within just two years the city bowed to public pressure and closed Platzspitz Park, which meant that addicts would be able to receive help at regular local clinics only.

Looking to
the Future

It is unlikely that the United States will completely shift its antidrug effort away from enforcement and into prevention and treatment. It is also unlikely that drugs will be legalized or even substantially decriminalized. There isn't the public support for such a move. In fact, 85 percent of the country is against legalizing drugs.

If anything, the government's war on drugs will probably put more pressure on attacking the foreign producers and high-level distributors. Street dealers and users won't be forgotten, but they probably won't be the chief target of the country's police forces either.

The future of America's drug treatment programs may be more difficult to evaluate. Funding is one factor. Moreover, it is difficult to determine the effectiveness of various programs. The most successful treatments appear to be those that make the addicts confront the reality of their habit, that they are no longer in control and need help. Once that happens, the chances of getting people off drugs improve sharply. As the country turns more of its attention toward reducing demand and preventing young people from getting involved, additional funds may become available for treatment centers, ensuring that these centers will play an even greater role in the war against drugs in the future.

Glossary

addiction A physiological need for a drug that is habit-forming.

amphetamine A drug that is a stimulant; causes the brain to speed up bodily functions, such as heart rate and blood pressure.

barbiturate A drug that is a depressant; causes the brain to slow down bodily functions.

cartel A combined business group.

counterculture A culture in which traditional values and behavior are rejected.

crack A chemically altered form of cocaine—a mixture of cocaine, baking soda, and water—that has more powerful effects than cocaine.

hallucination An imagined experience that feels very real.

hallucinogen A mind-altering drug that causes a person to see, hear, and feel things that are not real.

LSD A mind-altering drug; lysergic acid diethylamide.

PCP Phencylidine, a drug originally used as an anesthetic during surgery and now used by drug abusers seeking thrills and new experiences.

psychedelic A mind-altering drug that causes a person to perceive objects and sounds in a distorted way.

sedative A drug, such as a sleeping pill, that calms a person.

For Further Reading

Ball, Jacqueline A. *Everything You Need to Know About Drug Abuse.* New York: Rosen Group, 1992 (revised).

Freeman, Sally. *Drugs & Civilization.* New York: Chelsea House, 1988.

Hawkes, N. *International Drug Trade.* Vero Beach, FL: Rourke Corporation, 1988.

Monroe, Judy. *Drug Testing.* New York: Crestwood House, 1990.

Parker, Steve. *The Drug War.* New York: Franklin Watts, 1990.

Pearce, Jenny. *Colombia: The Drug War.* New York: Franklin Watts, 1990.

Terkel, Susan Neiberg. *Should Drugs Be Legalized?* New York: Franklin Watts, 1990.

Source Notes

Church, George J. "No Place to Run." *Time,* January 8, 1992, pp. 38–40.

Currie, Elliott. "Reckoning: Drugs, the Cities and the American Future." *Publishers Weekly,* November 16, 1992, pp. 51–52.

Falco, Mathea. *The Making of a Drug-Free America.* New York: Times Books, 1992.

Farley, Christopher John. "Hello Again, Mary Jane." *Time,* April 19, 1993, p. 59.

Friedman, Dorian. "How Clean Needles Are Saving Lives." *U.S. News & World Report,* March 29, 1993, p. 24.

Guyer, Rene. "Zurich's Needle Park." *Reader's Digest,* October 1991, pp. 136–138.

Hochman, Steve. "Heroin: Back on the Charts." *Rolling Stone,* September 17, 1992, p. 25.

Hodgson, Godfrey. *America in Our Time.* Garden City, NY: Doubleday, 1976.

Polson, Beth, and Newton, Miller, Ph.D. *Not My Kid: A Parent's Guide to Kids and Drugs.* New York: Arbor House, 1984.

Simon, Roger. "The Mayor Understood." *Newsweek,* August 27, 1990, p. 8.

Thompson, Dick. "Getting the Point in New Haven." *Time,* May 25, 1992, pp. 55–56.

White, Timothy. *Rock Lives—Profiles & Interviews.* New York: Henry Holt, 1992.

Index